Pudsey
in old picture postcards volume 1

by Ruth Strong

European Library

ISBN13: 978 90 288 3050 9

© 1985 European Library

© 2015 Reprint of the third edition of 2001

European Library Publishers

www.eurobib.nl

INTRODUCTION

'In no township – is the true West Riding type of character to be met with a greater natural strenght than at Pudsey.' So wrote a mid-19th century visitor to the town. Indeed Pudsey could be seen as epitomising the typical West Riding small textile town centred round 't' mill' and 'chapil'. The town's natural resources encouraged the early development of a local woollen industry. The district abounds in springs of soft water which flow into the becks which virtually surround the town. There is coal and stone locally too whilst the terrain, laying at the foothills of the pennines, is less inhospitable than more remote regions. Already by the 14th century woollen cloth was being made in the district. Subsequent expansion of the industry was encouraged by the availability of freehold land and by the town's proximity to the busy Leeds cloth market.

Pudsey's manorial background too encouraged its development as a textile town. The manor of 'Podechesaie' was mentioned in the 1084 Domesday Survey. For many years it was a sub-holding of the Calverley manor but during the Commonwealth Henry Calverley, a Royalist, was forced to sell much of his Pudsey property to help pay his fines. Eventually the manor itself was sold to a Pudsey man, Robert Milner. From the early 18th century, however, when the manor was inherited by Charles Milner of Preston Hall in Kent, there was little manorial control.

Pudsey's independent and pugnacious character was also nurtured by its ecclesiastical circumstances. Until the 19th century Pudsey was a chapelry within the extensive parish of Calverley and the Anglican Church's presence in the town was confined to a small chapel of ease. The tithes which Pudsey people had to pay towards the Calverley vicar's income, and the church rate paid towards the upkeep of the parish church fuelled resentment, making Pudsey fertile ground for religious nonconformity. Few towns had such a comprehensive spread of dissenting groups as Pudsey in the late 19th century. There were Congregationalists, Moravians, Wesleyans, Methodist New Connexion, Primitive Methodists, United Methodist Free Church, Baptists, Unitarians, Roman Catholics, the Salvation Army and Jehovah's witnesses. A by-product of the town's strong nonconformist tradition was its success in producing cricketers. Rivalry between the numerous Sunday Schools was expressed through the Sunday School Cricket League, which proved a rigorous nursery for aspiring young cricketers.

During the early 19th-century steam powered scribbling and fulling mills were established to serve Pudsey's many small independent cloth manufacturers. Weaving, however, continued to be on handlooms until the 1870s. The 1870s also saw the development of the local worsted, tanning, and boot and shoe manufacturing industries. As became a town of such industrial enterprise and success Pudsey received a Royal Charter of Incorporation in 1900 and for 74 years enjoyed the identity and prestige of its own mayor and corporation. In compiling this book is has been impossible to be unaware of the sense of civic 'progress' during the late 19th and early 20th centuries. Pudsey acquired its own Local Board of Health in 1872, a recreation ground in 1881, its own parliamentary division in 1885, a 'civic' fire engine in 1886, a public park in 1889, its incorporation as a borough in 1900, a Town Hall in 1912, a baby clinic and playground in 1928, and public baths in 1929. Each event was the occasion for great civic rejoicing. Finally, in 1937 Pudsey annexed the neighbouring Urban District Councils of Calverley and Farsley making the Pudsey Borough a buffer between the large County Boroughs of Leeds and Bradford.

But change came with local government reorganization in 1974. Overnight Pudsey's thousand year history as an independent manor, township and, lastly, borough, became irrelevant as the town became part of the huge new Metropolitan Borough of Leeds.

There have been changes in the town's industry too as the tanning, boot and shoe manufacturing and finally the textile industries declined. Today light engineering provides most local jobs, although the town has become largely a dormitory for those working elsewhere. The introduction of 'clean air' in the 1960s has transformed it into a desirable residential town, within five miles of both Leeds and Bradford and yet with a wealth of history and character of its own. This is ex-

pressed not least in its many 18th- and early 19th-century stone cottages. Those that survived slum clearance have now become highly desirable 'old weavers' cottages'. Tragically, however, most of Pudsey's old halls, the manor house, Acres Hall, the old parsonage, Littlemoor Hall and to a large extent Hutton Hall have all gone. Yet the town retains the unique 18th-century Moravian settlement at Fulneck and the lovely Cockersdale and Fulneck valleys are within a mile of most parts of the town.

Many of the best photographs in this book were taken around 1900. They were the work of members of the Pudsey and District Photographic Society, which included in its membership an optician, a plumber, a blacksmith and two doctors. Their technical expertise and inventive and artistic genius is reflected in their delightful photographs.

The following people and organizations have kindly loaned photographs: Fulneck Museum, Pudsey Civic Society, Pudsey Photographic Society, Jack Calvert, Barbara Holdsworth, Judy Holdsworth, Mary Moss, Roland Parker, Emily Read and Albert Taylor.

1. Pudsey was in the ancient parish of Calverley although at least since the 14th century it has had its own anglican chapel of ease. In 1824 this was replaced by St. Lawrence Church, seen here. The architect was Thomas Taylor who within 14 years designed 16 churches in West Yorkshire and East Lancashire. Pudsey Church is almost identical to Taylor's Holy Trinity at Huddersfield. The cost of £13,360 was met from a fund of £1,000,000 government money, used to build new churches in the growing industrial towns. Thomas Taylor always managed to acquire elevated sites for his churches and Pudsey is no exception. Its tower is a landmark for many miles in all directions. This picture was taken in about 1898. Today the young trees have matured, the blackened stonework cleaned and the 'table top' gravestones cleared and laid alongside the paths. This corner was the last site of the town stocks which had previously been under a large tree near the present Kings Arms. They were last used in 1851. The little girl in the photograph is Ethel Kershaw, the daughter of Dr. Kershaw of Radcliffe House (see 37).

CHAPELTOWN, PUDSEY

2. Chapeltown from the east. Chapeltown is so called because of the old anglican chapel of ease, laterly called All Saints, which once stood here. The long wall on the left of the photograph belonged to the chapel graveyard. This was not cleared until 1922 when the cenotaph was built. After St. Lawrence Church was consecrated in 1824 proposals to demolish the old chapel were strongly opposed so it, and its graveyard, were left to become increasingly derelict. In 1879 the Pudsey Local Board of Health's reluctance to clear the site led to a Local Government Enquiry which determined that the area should be cleared immediately. The Local Board therefore had the chapel quietly demolished during the night. There was such an uproar the following morning that the graveyard was left to decay even further for another 43 years.

3. This picture shows Ebenezer Primitive Methodist's two chapels in Richardshaw Lane. The 1835 chapel on the right, measuring just 11 yards by 8 yards, incorporated a cottage underneath which provided a useful income of £4 a year. In 1865 it became a private house, Ebenezer House, when the larger chapel on the left was built. The architect for the second chapel was Joseph Roberts of Farsley. Between the two chapels is the 1856 Sunday School which for many years was also used as a day school. It was replaced by a larger school in 1908. All three buildings were demolished about 15 years ago to make way for the new ring road. Ebenezer 'Prims' were great evangelists with their own brass band. They regularly campaigned at Pudsey feast, but their most memorable annual event was the Whit Sunday morning 'sing' when crowds would gather on Owlcotes at six in the morning to sing the Whitsuntide hymns.

4. Church Lane Wesleyan Chapel was dedicated by the President of the Methodist Conference, Reverend John Rattenbury in June 1861. The architect was John Kirk of Huddersfield and the cost £2,300. Six years later a Sunday School was built at the rear. The Wesleyans had sold their share in the Clock chapel in Wesley Square following the schism of the 1850s. For a time the Wesleyan congregation was small and without wealthy benefactors, so that the building of Church Lane chapel was largely a Circuit initiative. Soon however, new leaders in the town such as John Beer, a Bradford draper, W.D. Scales, James Stillings and Jonathan Webster, boot and shoe manufacturers, and John Ben Ward, a Bradford top maker, associated themselves with the Wesleyans. Church Lane chapel was closed in 1971 and the D.H.S.S. offices built on the site. The congregation moved to the old Primitive Methodist's chapel in Robin Lane which became St. Andrews Methodist Church. In 1982 St. Andrews was joined by the Methodists from Trinity chapel. (Trinity had replaced the Clock chapel in 1900.) So reunion within the Methodist Church was reflected in Pudsey with the coming together again after 130 years of the Wesleyans and Methodists.

5. Pudsey's United Reform Church is rightly proud of its long history. It originated in 1662 as a Presbyterian congregation (see 27), became 'Independent' in the 18th century and Congregationalist in the 19th century. Today the congregation is part of the United Reformed Church. The church seen here, built in 1864 at a cost of £2,500 was designed by Messrs. J.P. Pritchett and Son of Darlington. The firm designed many Congregational Churches in Yorkshire in the mid-19th century, all in the 'modern' neo-gothic style, most with a spire and transepts and many with a round St. Catherine's window as at Pudsey. In the 19th century Pudsey's Congregationalists set great store by education, opening a day school in 1853 and having a Mutual Improvement Society, Debating Society, adult classes and a lending library. One man to benefit greatly from this was Simeon Rayner who became the author of much of the late 19th century 'History of Pudsey'. The 1864 church was demolished in 1978 since when part of the Sunday School has been adapted for use as a church.

Opening of Primary Dept. Baptist Church, Pudsey

6. This delightful group is posing outside the Baptist's first chapel in Pudsey, built in 1851 at Littlemoor. By the 1890s such a small chapel was considered 'unworthy' of Pudsey and so, with help from Farsley Baptists a large new chapel was built in 1897 on adjoining land. The old chapel was then adapted for use as the Sunday School and opened in about 1898. This neat little building has recently been demolished. However did the women manage to balance those enormous hats? Even some of the children are wearing them. The older women too seem to vie with each other for the most elaborate bonnets.

7. Radcliffe Lane Sunday School. Perhaps this photograph was taken following the opening of Pudsey Church's new Radcliffe Lane Sunday School on Easter Monday, 1893, when a procession of over 500 had walked from the church to the new school singing 'Onward Christian Soldiers'. The architect was Charles Sebastian Nelson of Fulneck who designed many local buildings in the late 19th century, and the cost just over £2,000. Some years later an extension for the primary was made at the back. The building incorporates the foundation stone of an earlier Sunday School, built in 1831 on the same site. Before that the Church Sunday School had squeezed into the Old Town School which still stands at the top of Valley Road.

8. Lowtown, looking towards 'Druggist's Corner'. There have been a few changes in Lowtown in the 80 or so years since this picture was taken. The spire of the Mechanics Institute, now the Town Hall, was taken down about 20 years ago when it became unsafe. About the same time Commercial Buildings, in the centre distance, was replaced by modern, single-storeyed shops. In 1906 the Commercial Building tenants were James Galloway, grocer, John William Crabtree, glass and china dealer, Samuel Robinson, confectioner, newsagent and stationer and Harry Lister, tailor and outfitter. Beyond was William Bennett and Sons, grocers and horse corn dealers. The three-storeyed building adjoining the Mechanics Institute was built by the Leeds Industrial Cooperative Society in 1871, nine years before the Mechanics Institute. Planned by Wilson and Bailey of Leeds it was the first architect designed building in the town centre. Across the road is James Booth's, grocers and 'Corn and Straw Merchant'. The old sign is just visible.

9. Lowtown 'Coop' grocery department in 1899. The Leeds Cooperative Flour and Provision Society opened their first 'provision' store in Pudsey in 1859. It moved to the new store seen here in 1873 where it remains today. Soon two more grocery shops were opened at Greenside and Littlemoor. By 1882 the three shops had an annual turnover of £20,000 so must have had a good share of the town's custom. The two boys who look to us very young to be working would probably be part-timers. Pudsey was known for the early age at which it allowed its schoolchildren to work part-time. The determining factor was the number of school attendances, a system well designed to ease the work of the school attendance officer.

10. Manor House Street shortly after 1900. The street took its name from Pudsey's manor house, which, until 1910, stood immediately behind where the photographer is standing (see 26). On the extreme right is the old Black Bull with the vine, the traditional sign that wine was for sale, hanging outside. This is one of Pudsey's oldest inns. Double fronted and three storeys high (a 'garret house') it was similar in design to Pudsey's other 18th-century inns, the Traveller's Rest at Fartown, the Fulneck Inn and the original Golden Lion. During the 19th century the Black Bull was host to many Reform Association Annual Dinners. It was replaced by the present building about 35 years ago. In the distance is James Booth's shop. The old buildings behind, previously known as Hammerton Fold, but now called Booths Yard, have recently been sympathetically converted into an attractive shopping precinct.

11. 'Druggist's Corner' looking up Lidget Hill, possibly about 1910. Many people remember the centre of Pudsey as 'Galloway's Corner' as for more than 50 years James Galloway's family kept the grocer's shop at the bottom left hand corner of the picture. However, before that the shop belonged to a chemist, Joseph Walker, hence the old name 'Druggist's Corner'. Joseph Walker's services were manifold: he extracted teeth and supplied 'Artificial Mineral Teeth' at 9/- and 15/6, stocked 'Twelve Tree Bug Destroyer' for bedroom pests, and crochet patterns, 'the most original ever in Pudsey'. His 'Infant Preservative' cost 7½d a bottle. He was also a printer and for five years President of the Mechanics Institute. No wonder the centre of the town was called after him. Immediately behind his shop was Sykes Crowther's blacksmith's shop. The wooden hut beyond was Mrs. Ross' tripe shop where the warmth from the coke stove was a great attraction on cold winter nights.

12. This is one of a cluster of ramshackle huts which were cleared from the remnant of the old Waver Green in 1889 making way for the present Midland Bank. There was Job Wilcock's (Job Cock) 'pey 'oil', where a basin of pea soup cost a penny, Tripey Ross' tripe shop, the town's first fried fish shop and, surprisingly, Brayshaw's photographic studio. Being in the town centre it was also a 'cal 'oil' for catching up on local gossip. In the 1880s there were plenty of newly redundant handloom weavers with time on their hands. These huts stood on the site of the Waver Green pond which in 1851 was filled in because of its 'noxious exhalations'. On the right is the Local Board office, approached from outside by a flight of steps. Below was the fire engine room and in front stood a trough with an old iron pump. Additional Local Board offices (now Pudsey House) were built in 1882 in Crawshaw Field. The older offices seen here were demolished in 1903 and Pudsey's main Post Office built on the site.

13. The building on the left was built in 1903 as Pudsey's new Post Office (see 12). An earlier Post Office on Lidget Hill (down two steps at the end of The Ivies) was presided over for nearly 50 years by the formidable postmaster, Henry Gott. He was perhaps the best known man in the town, acting as 'general adviser to all and sundry on any subject' and even making wills when required. On the right is Commercial Buildings (see 8). The trees immediately beyond are in the garden of Greenbank, the home of Dr. Byrd, who always visited his patients by bicycle. Beyond the next row of shops the grounds of Toft House reach down to the road. In 1910 this was considered as a possible site for a Town Hall rather than adapting the Mechanics Institute building on Waver Green. The Fulneck architect, Charles Sebastian Nelson strongly urged the Toft House site. It was much the larger of the two with room not only for a Town Hall but also a library, public baths and art gallery. Perhaps unfortunately Mr. Nelson's plea went unheeled by the Town Council. Behind the far tram is Church Lane Wesleyan chapel (see 4).

CHURCH LANE, PUDSEY.

RELIABLE SERIES 765/43

14. Church Lane, looking east towards Druggist's Corner. Before St. Lawrence Church was built in 1824 Church Lane was called Chapel Lane because it led to the old anglican chapel of ease at Chapeltown (see 2). On the left is the boundary wall of Church Lane Wesleyan chapel (see 4). Below the row of cottages on the right is the old Rate Office and Borough Surveyor's Department. This was demolished about 20 years ago and the new Library built on the site. The cottages below the Rate Office too have gone making way for new shops and an enlarged market place. The errand boys in the foreground suggest that the picture was taken on a weekday, yet the road is quite empty. Apart from a tram rattling passed every half hour or so the only transport would be horses and carts, which, according to the evidence in the picture, trundled down the middle of the road.

15. Here is a better view of the old Rate Office. The man on the right is John Huggan, the Rate Office accountant. The Borough Surveyors Department and the Rate Office moved to the Town Hall when it was opened in 1912. These premises were then occupied for many years by the Leeds Provincial Building Society which moved here from Manor House Street. Behind the Rate Office was Stansfield Square. Similar squares, yards and folds, usually named after the men who built them, were typical of Pudsey's 19th century housing.

16. This photograph of Church Lane, looking west, was taken before the trams came in 1908. Today the row of cottages in the distance where Mrs. Parker had a little confectioner's shop has been replaced by modern houses. The high wall and trees of the Congregational Church Manse garden beyond too have gone. In the right foreground is the Park Hotel, then only recently having changed its name from the New Inn. About time too as it had already been an inn for over 75 years. The original two-storeyed house had been built by Benjamin Farrer, a local yeoman clothier, in 1734. The lintel over the door still has the lettering F / B E / 1734. In 1833 it was bought by two brothers called Northrop. It was already an inn and had had an upper storey added. The brothers subsequently built on the land to the west of the inn. This is still called Northrop's Yard. In the 1880s when St. Lawrence Cricket Club had its ground across the road on what is now the park, the New Inn made a convenient club house, although the club also had a pavilion on the ground, built in the new white glazed brickwork. The New Inn was also the first meeting place of St. Lawrence Masonic Lodge.

CHURCH LANE, PUDSEY.

RELIABLE SERIES 765/42

17. This is the same stretch of Church Lane as No. 16 but looking in the opposite direction and taken after the trams came in 1908. The spire on the right, since taken down as unsafe, belongs to the Unitarian Church. This was built in 1861 to designs of William Hill of Leeds. It was the first gothic style nonconformist chapel in Pudsey. The Pudsey Unitarians developed from the Barkerite secession from Mount Zion Methodist New Connexion chapel in 1841. The Pudsey Barkerites drifted towards Unitarianism and were eventually taken under the wing of the Leeds Unitarians who helped in the building of the chapel. The woman on the pavement is wearing a heavy black shawl, probably with tassels round the edge, reaching almost to the ground. Many women wore shawls. A shawl was quite warm and a lot cheaper than a coat.

18. Chapeltown looking east from the Commercial Hotel. On the left is Parker's watchmaker and jewellers shop. It was built in the 18th century, probably originally as an inn. The clock and watchmaker William Potts began business here in 1834. He moved to Leeds in the early 1860s but retained his Pudsey connections. In 1865 he supplied Pudsey Church's new £200 clock, with 'Westminster chimes' and today William Potts & Sons Ltd. of Leeds still services the church clock. The Pudsey shop was taken by Joseph Parker and his family continued the business in the same premises until they were demolished in 1931. The house facing up Chapeltown belonged to 'Havercake Wilson', famous for his oatcakes (or havercakes) which he hawked round the town with a basketful on each arm. Just to the right is the boundary wall of the old graveyard (see 2). In 1908 the area in the foreground became the tram terminus. At first there was only room for one tram, the nearest passing place being by the old graveyard. Within a few years however, the garden wall on the left was taken down making room for the track to divide to accommodate two trams. The Congregational Church is on the right (see 5).

19. Pudsey looks a very dreary place from this photograph of Station Street taken round about 1900. As there were less houses than today so there were fewer gardens and trees, whilst over all hung a pall of smoke from Pudsey's many mill chimneys. On the far left is the Royal Hotel, possibly the only purpose built public house in the town. It was built by Joseph Beaumont of Hutton Hall (see 27) in 1879, the year Greenside station was opened. It was obviously intended as a station hotel. However there already was a Railway Inn, which had been built in 1847 when there had been abortive plans to make a railway between Leeds and Pudsey Littlemoor. Notice the stone 'crossing' over the road in the foreground. One of the first improvements made by Pudsey's new Local Board of Health in 1872 was to provide continuations of the causeways, or 'crossings' over the muddy roads. The cottages on the left were destroyed by a high explosive bomb during the Second World War. A second bomb was dropped near the Fox and Grapes at the other end of the railway tunnel, suggesting that the intention may have been to block the line.

20. This part of Littlemoor Road has changed little in the last 70 years. Clarendon Buildings on the left was then newly built. At the far end William Glover was in business as a 'fruit and fish merchant'. Locally he was known as Billy Chuck and was especially popular with children as he had a small cart from which he sold ice cream guaranteed 'morning gathered'. You can see the barber's pole of John Jessop's, hairdresser and tobacconist. The row of cottages in the distance, now Woodfield Terrace, was formerly known as 'Bob Spencers Row'. In 1868 Robert Spencer built Brick Mill, a woollen mill beyond the houses on the right and presumably bought this row of ten cottages for his handloom weavers. They had been built in the early 19th century with all the privies at the bottom of the row, a long way away on a wet night for those living at the top. The street sign for Crowthers Yard would be one of 50 such plates provided by the Local Board in 1886 at 4/6 (22½p) each. Made of caste iron the border and lettering were gilded.

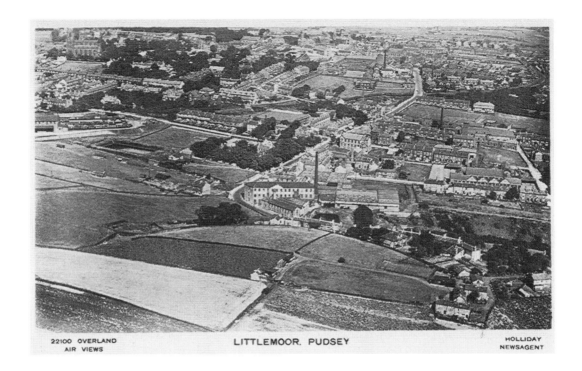

22100 OVERLAND
AIR VIEWS

LITTLEMOOR. PUDSEY

HOLLIDAY
NEWSAGENT

21. The stretch of Littlemoor Road and Robin Lane seen in No. 20 is included in this aerial photograph of the early 1920s. Clarendon Buildings and Spencers Row are easily identified. Cliff Mill in the foreground, dating from 1837, was originally one of Pudsey's numerous company mills for scribbling and fulling woollen cloth. The Woolpack Inn, closed in 1937, used to be just behind the mill. Above and slightly to the left of Cliff Mill Littlemoor Hall (see 29) can just be seen in the trees. Further up Robin Lane on the left is Crawshaw House, standing rather starkly in the middle of a field where Crawshaw Park and Crawshaw Rise are today. It was built between 1820 and 1845 by William Beaumont, who was that unusual local phenomenon, a cloth manufacturer who was also a Tory. In 1846 he sent a piece of his own superfine cloth, 'the finest ever made up in Yorkshire' to Sir Robert Peel 'as a thank offering for his noble and spirited exertions in abolishing the corn laws'.

22. Fulneck Moravian settlement looking west. The Moravian Church originated in Bohemia in the 15th century, about 100 years before the Reformation. It quickly spread to Moravia from where the church takes its name. During the religious revival of the early 18th century the Moravians came to know the English evangelist, Benjamin Ingham. In 1742 they took over about 40 of his religious societies to the west of Leeds. At least one of these was in Pudsey. Two years later Benjamin Ingham bought the 22 acre Fallneck estate, on Pudsey's southern boundary, as a centre for the Moravians' work in Yorkshire. The Moravians changed the name to Lambshill, and later to Fulneck after a historic town in Moravia. The settlement grew up along the main street leaving the rest of the estate as agricultural land. Today Fulneck village survives as a local oasis almost untouched by the busyness of the 19th and 20th centuries. On the left is the main terrace, facing south over Fulneck valley. The original congregation inn is in the distance. The bay windowed house on the right, 'Nelson House', was the home of the architect Charles Sebastian Nelson whose work included many local chapels, Sunday Schools and mills.

23. This picture shows much the same part of the Fulneck street as No. 22 only looking east. In the centre distance on the left are the backs of the cottages seen in No. 25. By 1748 the main part of the costly chapel, the large building in the right foreground, was finished. At first the Moravians called it Grace Hall. The two-storeyed porch, built of poorer quality local stone, and the cupula, were added in 1779. Over the years houses for the single sisters, the single brethren, the minister, the widows and for the girls' and boys' schools were built along the same contour. In the 1920s the last gap was filled completing the continuous terrace, with a glorious southerly outlook over Fulneck valley.

24. Here is a better picture of the Fulneck inn seen in the distance in No. 22. There has been an inn at Fulneck since 1761 although the building seen here dates from 1771. As Fulneck was the centre for Moravians from a wide area the need for an inn was obvious. The level horseshoe shaped area in front was made for vehicles such as carriages and waggonettes to turn round. The inn's proximity to the single brethrens' house was a constant anxiety. One precaution was to stop the brethren going to the inn to be shaved. With the coming of the temperance movement in the 1830s the inn became a Temperance Hotel, the innkeeper, William Lister, being allowed a reduction in rent in lieu of the financial loss. By 1900 the hotel had become The Morningside Guest House. Later still it became the Boys' School music department. In 1968 the cottages below were pulled down and foundations dug for a new science block. Unfortunately this allowed the foundations of the old inn to shift and on Christmas Eve the building collapsed.

25. These children, in their Sunday best, are posing outside the home of Charles Mazzini Gaunt at 43 Fulneck. Charles Mazzini's father had walked daily from Drighlington to Pudsey to learn the tailoring trade. However, he managed to send Charles Mazzini to London for his apprenticeship. Charles Mazzini then began his own business at Fulneck End. He was remembered as 'a merry boy', a favourite outing being to walk with his friend Dr. Squires across the valley to the Greyhound at Tong. Both wore distinctive square hats which they had specially made in Leeds. Charles Mazzini's daughter, Alice, is standing in the doorway. The little boy on the right is Hugh Brook who recently published his memories of old Fulneck in 'I Remember, I Remember'. The cobbled steps originally led to the Moravian's windmill on the hilltop, used for grinding corn. The road down the far side is still called Mill Hill. These cottages were demolished in 1912 to make way for the new Boys Brigade Headquarters. The two farthest cottages in the distance now house the Fulneck museum.

26. The north front of Pudsey's manor house, shortly before it was demolished in 1910 to make way for the Manor Hall. Drawings of the south front and observations by the architect William Shackleton made as it was pulled down suggest that part of the house, including a fine transomed and mullioned window, was Elizabethan. It was apparently enlarged early in the 18th century by John Milner whose initials were said 'plainly to be seen' on the north gable of the west bay. John Milner's father had bought the Pudsey manor from Walter Calverley in 1663. In 1724 the manor passed to John's second son, Charles, who lived in Kent. Thereafter the manor house was let and later divided into cottages. In 1867 the building became separated from the manor when it was bought by Mr. George Hinings of Littlemoor Hall. One of the tenants during the 1870s was 'The British Workman', a temperance 'public house'. Over the door was the inscription: 'Here men may sit, read and think, then safely home return.' It did not survive very long! Latterly the tenements became business premises as seen in this photograph.

27. In the 17th century this was the largest house in Pudsey being taxed on 7 hearths. There was a hall, parlour, 'Dineing Room', two kitchens and five 'Chambers' as well as a study housing £50 worth of books. The study was probably over the gabled porch. It was the home of Mr. James Sale, who was one of about 2,000 Presbyterians and others who were expelled from the Anglican Church in 1662. Thereafter Pudsey Presbyterians met at his house which in 1672 became licensed as Pudsey's first dissentors' meeting house. Pudsey's Presbyterians developed via Independants and Congregationalists to become the present United Reformed Church. On the death of James Sales' widow the house passed to the Hutton family, Richard Hutton was James Sales' son-in-law, and for many years was known as Hutton Hall. When this photograph was taken about 60 years ago the west end of the house was in the process of being demolished. Sadly today even less remains of this historic house.

28. Acres Hall. This rambling old farmhouse stood just below the present Acres Hall Crescent. For many years it was owned by the Hutchinson family and old people still remember the adjoining land as 'Hutchinson's Fields'. At the beginning of the 19th century the Pudsey-born surgeon William Hey, the founder of Leeds Infirmary, recommended that the nearby well of exceptionally soft water should be developed as a spa. There is no record of his advice being followed! In the early 20th century Acres Hall, then occupied by Benjamin Glover, was one of the houses where Valley Road Wesleyans used to sing on the Whit Monday walk. Later it was divided into cottages, as seen in this photograph, and eventually replaced by a modern house. But some of the timbers from the old hall seem to have been used in some nearby fencing. These suggest that the house had once been timber framed.

29. Littlemoor Hall, an elegant, sashed house, was built in about 1740 by William Moss, a prosperous Pudsey maltster. It was an early home for the Moravian Single Sisters before the Fulneck Sisters' House was built in 1752 and was again used by the Single Sisters between 1767 and 1794 as an annex to the Sisters' House. The Sisters had perpetual trouble as they walked to and from their meetings at Fulneck from 'wicked lads from Pudsey throwing stones and dirt and calling in a very abusive manner'. In 1861 the 20 acre estate was broken up and sold, a 'New Street' being laid down the middle of the plots. The house was bought by Mr. George Hinings, a draper and silk mercer, later passing to members of the Huggan family. This fine example of early Georgian domestic architecture was demolished about 20 years ago.

30. Toft House, which stood behind the present Post Office, was built in the early 19th century by Samuel Sharp. He described himself as 'yeoman' although his business interests were legion. He had shares in the Albion scribbling and fulling mill, owned a brewery, at least 50 houses, and farmed 70 acres. Rather ostentiously he referred to his house, set in ornamental gardens, as a 'Mansion'. The field in which Toft House was built had been called Toft, hence the name. There were many 'Toft' field names in the area between Back Lane (now Cemetery Road), Chapeltown and Church Lane. These took their name from the 'Toftfield', one of Pudsey's open fields mentioned in the 14th century Calverley Charters. Toft House was demolished about 20 years ago.

31. This old house, which until about 20 years ago stood almost opposite Pudsey Church lych gate was, in 1826, the scene of a long remembered tragedy. One night the occupant, Mr. Thomas Fairfax Carlyle, whilst asleep in bed heard suspicious noises. Grabbing the sword which he habitually kept by the bedside he went downstairs, and seeing a figure outside standing on the parlour window sill thrust his sword through the window. This mortally wounded the intruder who turned out to be his daughter's lover, Joseph Blackburn. Mr. Carlyle was tried at York on a charge of manslaughter but found 'Not Guilty', the judge considering he had 'acted... as any man possessed of a certain nerve would have done'. The inscription on Joseph Blackburn's tombstone in Pudsey Church yard reads: *Sharp was the stroke that did appear,/ Which took my life away,/ O reader, then for Heaven prepare,/ On earth you cannot stay./ The moon gave light, he took sight,/ Through the top pane I lost my life.*

32. This large cloth manufacturer's house is said to have been built in 1711 although its style suggests that it was rather later. It was still there in 1908, 23 years after Greenside Council School, seen in the background, was built. It must have made the school extremely dark. The house may well have once been the home of a woolstapler such as John Hutchinson who lived in Chapeltown in the mid-18th century. He had an annual contract with a Beverley farmer for wool which he then sold to local handloom weavers. The filled in doorway in the garret, the usual name for the top storey, would be used to hoist in the bales of wool. Latterly the building became Rankin's, and then Illingworth's, grocers and off-license.

33. This old couple, posing in their cottage garden at Buffy Lump in about 1900, was probably considered by the photographer an 'old world' scene even then. The cottage is shown on the 1817 Enclosure map, standing near Smalewell Mill on the Pudsey upper moor before it was enclosed. Surprisingly it survives, almost unaltered, today. It is built of local sandstone from Uppermoor quarry with the corner stones set vertically for extra strength. The roof, of heavy flagstone slabs, making a gentle pitch essential, is typical of local roofing before lighter forms of slating became available. Notice the two butts. Most cottages without their own well and some way from a public well had a water butt fed with rainwater from the guttering. Perhaps the other butt was for storing 'old wesh', or urine. This was bought by local mills for scouring cloth.

34. Here is Jim Walker outside his greengrocers shop in Lowtown which he kept from 1898 until his death 35 years later. He also had a drapers shop next door and the Lowtown Post Office next to that. You could take a jam jar for ¾d worth of golden syrup, filled from a tap, or buy a pair of kippers for 2d. But his speciality was his ice-cream which he made himself in the tub in the picture. The lining of the tub was filled with ice, then fresh milk and eggs were put in the inner container and churned until it changed into ice-cream. Jim Walker's ice-cream was recommended by doctors for children who had had their tonsils out, (usually on the kitchen table). People walking down Lowtown to watch the matches at Britannia cricket ground were also good customers.

35. In 1910 part of George Verity's large new building for his Lowtown house furnishing and undertaking business was gutted by fire. Here are some of the 'thousands' who came the following day to wonder at the damage. Latterly George Verity had converted part of the upper storey into a roller skating rink. He installed an American maple floor, a band, a uniformed manager from Hunslet, and called it the Olympia. However, the novelty soon evaporated and the week following the fire it was to have been reopened by a cinematograph company. After the fire the damaged part was rebuilt in a different style from the remainder of the block and opened as the Palace Picture House. Seats were 2d, 4d and 6d, the most expensive being downstairs at the front, like the stalls at the theatre. Today the Pasadena Social Club occupies the premises.

36. William Henry Beaumont's butcher's shop at 35 Chapeltown. Until well into this century all Pudsey butchers killed their own beasts. Each Tuesday the cattle were driven up from Leeds cattle market by Henry Haley whose shouting to urge the animals up the last hill into Pudsey became a familiar sound. As he drove them up Lowtown, along Robin Lane, up Fartown and along to Greenside and Chapeltown he dropped beasts off at the various butchers. In 1900 there were no less than 21 butchers in the town. The number of slaughter houses was a continuing concern to the Medical Officer of Health. Many opened straight onto the street and killing day always attracted crowds of children. This was especially so as most butchers seemed to rely on the enthusiastic help of young boys pulling on a rope to immobilise the beast whilst the butcher struck it with a pole axe. Today a modern row of shops stands on this site.

37. This well turned out horse and trap was used by Dr. Kershaw for visiting his patients. Sometimes he was driven by his groom, seen here, although he often drove himself with his little daughter, Ethel, sitting alongside him. The photograph is taken in Radcliffe Lane. Radcliffe House where Dr. Kershaw lived is behind the trees on the left. It was built in the early 18th century and was the childhood home of William Hey who was to become a famous surgeon, the founder of Leeds Infirmary and mayor of Leeds. His sister, Dorothy, continued to live in the house after her marriage to John Radcliffe. Gradually the house acquired the name 'Radcliffe House' and the adjoining lane became known as 'Radcliffe Lane'. Radcliffe House then became a doctor's house for almost 150 years. Dr. Machill, Dr. Mumford, Dr. Kershaw, Dr. Brown, Dr. Ackroyd and Dr. Allan all lived here. Dr. Kershaw employed a Mr. Rushforth to visit his patients each Friday night to collect what they could afford to pay for his services, perhaps 2d or 3d a week.

38. This photograph must have been taken before 1906 as by then John Webster's shop was also the Waterloo Post Office. Before that the Post Office was a few doors to the left. Pudsey then had a very efficient postal service. At Waterloo, one of 12 sub Post Offices in the town, there were four daily clearances of the post box and three daily deliveries. The picture shows two drays, heavily ladened with corn, or perhaps flour, each of which takes three horses to draw it. John Webster and his helpers are ready to heave the sacks into the first floor warehouse. There was still a steady demand for horse corn before the advent of motor-cars. Apparently there was also still a market for malt and hops showing that some people still brewed their own beer, or 'drink'.

22104 OVERLAND AIR VIEWS   WATERLOO, PUDSEY   HOLLIDAY NEWSAGENT

39. Pudsey still looks quite rural in this picture taken in the early 1920s, shortly after the Waterloo housing estate was built. Until the enclosure of the commons in 1819 most of the land sloping towards the camera was part of Pudsey's upper moor. Exceptions were part of Gibraltar, or Delf End, seen in the bottom right corner of the photograph (see 40), and 22 acres, roughly where Waterloo estate was later built. The latter was enclosed from the moor in 1705 to provide an income for the curate at Pudsey's anglican chapel of ease. At the bottom left corner of the estate is St. James' first purpose built church. St. James had originated as a mission from Pudsey St. Lawrence in the late 19th century, at first using an old corrugated iron hut. Bradley Lane, running from opposite St. James' church to Gibraltar, is probably named after John Bradley who in the mid-19th century lived adjoining the lane.

40. The hamlet of Delf End, or Gibraltar, in 1897. This hamlet developed in the 18th century as a cluster of cottages on Pudsey moor, held on long leases from Pudsey's lord of the manor. Some of these cottages are in the bottom left hand corner of the photograph. In 1801 Joseph Thackrah of Woodhall, and Thomas Fairfax Carlyle (see 31) similarly leased part of the moor to build Gibraltar Mill in the valley below. It was Pudsey's second steam-powered scribbling and fulling mill (the first was Union Bridge Mill in Roker Lane), and until the mid-19th century was also the largest. It was notable as being one of the first mills in the Leeds district to install gas lighting. Following the enclosure of Pudsey moor in 1819 Joseph Thackrah acquired a small plot above Delf End on which he built the 'Upper Mill', seen here. Mr. Carlyle had by then left the firm as a bankrupt. The cottages on the right were later built for handloom weavers. The Upper Mill was not rebuilt after being destroyed by fire in 1897 but the remaining part of the mill was subsequently bought by James Womersley and worked for many years in conjunction with Smalewell Mill by his sons Daniel and Stafford.

41. Mary Moorhouse's shop at 54 Gibraltar was just off the bottom left hand corner of No. 40. She seems to have kept about everything that the 200 or so inhabitants of the mill hamlet of Gibraltar, or Delph End, could possibly ask for. As well as being a grocer and draper she was licensed to sell beer, porter and tobacco, and a close look at her window shows she also stocked teapots, cooking pots, miscellaneous ornaments and pictures, and lace. Notice the carefully carved lettering over the shop window. The shop was later kept by 'Cider Annie', but as Gibraltar Mill declined and eventually closed so the hamlet contracted and the customers left. The shop was closed about 15 years ago. Mary Moorhouse makes a trim figure standing in her doorway with a leg o' mutton sleeved blouse, stays at their most constricting and a brilliant white apron. Perhaps she was dressed especially for the occasion.

42. This photograph of mill girls at Crawshaw mill, with the overlooker in the middle, was taken in 1906. It was then a worsted spinning mill, in 1899 employing nearly 200 of which, 'Some do doff, and some do spin, and some do put the rovings in.' The hours were 6 a.m. to 5.30 p.m. and the pay about 5/- (or 25 pence) a week. The business belonged to Messrs. Lund Bros. Alfred and Thomas Lund had begun with just a dozen spinning frames renting 'room and power' at Crawshaw mill. As the business prospered they took the whole of the mill. Both became great benefactors to the town, Thomas giving large financial support to Trinity Methodists and Alfred to Pudsey Church. For many years Alfred Lund lived at Grove House. In 1928 his widow became Pudsey's first woman mayor. Crawshaw mill had been built in 1831 as a 'Company Mill', owned by 50 Pudsey clothiers, or small cloth manufacturers. Virtually all were political 'Reformers' and to celebrate the repeal of the Corn Laws in 1846 a monster plum pudding was mixed, and boiled, in the mill dye pan. The pudding was paraded through the streets on a wherry and later consumed by the hundreds who crowded into the mill field.

43. The fire engine on the right was bought by Pudsey Corporation in 1917 for £1,200. It was called the 'John Keighley' after the chairman of the Fire Brigade Committee. As it proved too large to negotiate all the town's steep hills the mayor, Sir William Forrest, gave a smaller engine, seen on the left. To accommodate the two new engines, the old municipal offices on Waver Green were altered to provide a spacious Fire Station. Recently the building has again been altered and is now Pudsey House. Pudsey had had a voluntary fire brigade since the early 19th century which in 1886 was taken over by Pudsey's Local Board of Health. At this time the engine was steam-powered, the fire being lighted and the steam pressure raised as the engine was horse-drawn to the fire. But for many years the old hand machine continued to be used if the horses were slow in coming (see 56). There were always plenty of willing hands to pull the engine to the scene of the fire and then to man the pumps.

44. Stanningley Station. A prelude to a day at the seaside. The railway was late in coming to Pudsey. The first line between Leeds and Bradford, opened in 1846, ran along the Aire valley. In 1854 the Leeds, Bradford and Halifax Junction Railway opened a direct route with a station at Stanningley. Pudsey, however, had to wait until 1878 for a branch from Stanningley joining it to the main line. Pudsey had to wait longer still for a direct line to Leeds. Even then most excursion trains still only collected passengers on the main line. So Pudsey's Whit Tuesday Choir Trips, its Sunday School and Band of Hope outings, and its Mechanics Institute and Church Institute excursions usually began at Stanningley station. And ended with a long pull up Richardshaw Lane.

45. Pudsey Greenside Station would be just 19 years old when this photograph was taken in 1897. To celebrate its opening on 1st April 1878 the Pudsey Brass Band paraded through the town and the church bells rung throughout the day. Pudsey's other station, at Lowtown, was opened a few months later. As the route to Bradford was not opened until 1892, for 14 years Pudsey Greenside was the end of the line. At first it had just 16 trains a day but by 1900 this had increased to 60. A return to Leeds cost 1/6 first class, 1/- second class and 9d third class. Waggons loaded with bales of wool for local mills were shunted into the large goods depot on the right of the picture to be unloaded and the bales stored awaiting collection. The line was closed in the 1960s.

46. After much pressure from Pudsey's Local Board of Health the railway from Leeds to Pudsey Greenside was extended in 1892 to rejoin the main Leeds to Bradford line at Laisterdyke. It was a difficult and expensive line to construct involving a tunnel a quarter of a mile long and a massive embankment, said to be the highest in England. It took three years to build and claimed the lives of at least two navvies. The Pudsey Vicar, Mr. Copeland, responded to the need of so many workers lodging in the town by opening a Pudsey Navvy Mission. Many of the Irish navvies settled in Pudsey where there had been a Roman Catholic Church since 1884. This picture shows a train from Bradford steaming along the embankment towards Greenside tunnel.

47. This picture was taken during the official opening of the tramline from Stanningley to Pudsey Chapeltown in June 1908. The bedecked tram makes its stately way up Church Lane, preceded by members of the Pudsey Council. Standing on the tram's upper deck are the mayor and mayoress, Councillor and Mrs. George Huggan. The track had been tested some days previously when school children were given free rides to Stanningley bottom. Many forgot they had to walk back and so got caned for being late for school. Before trams had linked Stanningley with Leeds and Bradford every Saturday crowds of Stanningley and Farsley people had walked up Richardshaw Lane to spend their money in Pudsey. The trams had changed all that. Now that spenders could ride up the hill to Pudsey for 1d it was hoped Pudsey would get its trade back again. The garden wall on the left belongs to Toft House (see 30). Pudsey Picture House, later Fine Fare, was built here. The cottages on the right were demolished to enlarge the market place.

48. Pudsey's first Conservative Club, seen here, was opened in 1880. £600 was raised on the share system to buy property opposite the old graveyard in Chapeltown. Another £300 was spent on converting the cottages into a comfortable club house, complete with 'a really splendid' billiard room. When the nearby Church Institute closed in 1895 the Conservative Club membership soared. In 1899 therefore a new club house, the present building, was built on the same site. Most of the town's conservative support in the 19th century was at the Chapeltown end, or the 'top end' of the town. The 'low end' was a liberal and nonconformist stronghold. Hugh Proctor, seen standing in the old club doorway, had been a handloom weaver. He would be one of many thrown out of work with the introduction of power looms in local woollen mills in the 1870s.

PUDSEY ST LAWRENCE C C

49. Pudsey St. Lawrence Cricket Club team about 1910. Pudsey is perhaps best known for its cricketers. It has two main Clubs, St. Lawrence, established in 1846 and Britannia in 1854. For many years their grounds were adjacent to each other on what is now Pudsey park and playground. Britannia's field was bought by Pudsey's Local Board of Health in 1879, to become the town's recreation ground. Britannia still rented it for practices and matches, but not between August 16th and 28th when Pudsey feast took over. The Club later moved to its present ground at Lowtown. In 1889 St. Lawrence too was forced to move when the Local Board bought their field for the park. St. Lawrence's new ground, the present one, was at Tofts Road. This picture contains many well-known names. The first three from the left on the back row are Frank Wilson, W. Hobson and J.W. Lawson. The president, Sir Walter Forrest, wears a boater. The captain, Richard Ingham, is on his left. Major Booth is on the extreme right. On the right of the front row is Henry Hutton, the father of Leonard, whilst in the middle is the 15 year old Herbert Sutcliffe. Herbert Sutcliffe's first match with Pudsey St. Lawrence is still remembered. He played in short trousers and batting at No. 6 saved the match. The captain, Richard Ingham, said to him afterwards: 'Play like that lad and one day you'll play for England.'

50. Pudsey park lake. The opening of Pudsey park in October 1889 was spectacular. The procession represented all aspects of the town including the Local Board, School Board, Burial Board, Board of Guardian, Pudsey Gas and Water Companies, the Mechanics Institute, local postal services and political clubs. Led by Pudsey Brass Band and the Ebenezer Primitive Methodist Band the procession wound its way round the Mechanics Institute (the town's most impressive non-denominational building) and up to the Church Lane entrance to the park. Here Mr. Briggs Priestley, M.P. for the Pudsey Division, opened the gates with a solid silver key. The speech making was perforce cut short due to the 'enormous – pressure of the crowd'. The crowds returned in the evening to see the illuminations and the best firework display ever seen in Pudsey. The photograph shows the park just eight years old. The land had previously been St. Lawrence Cricket ground. The pond was filled in about 40 years ago and the site imaginatively transformed into an extensive rock garden with a network of twisting paths and bridges which delighted thousands of small children. Today it is a rose garden.

51. Pudsey park bandstand about 1900. The park's elegant bandstand was given by Mr. Briggs Priestley M.P. when he opened the park in 1889. It was designed by Charles Sebastian Nelson who was also the architect for the park lodge. Soon the sound of brass band music coming from the park became part of the atmosphere of summer Sunday afternoons. Other gifts for the new park included a 'handsome drinking fountain', complete with goblet, given by W.D. Scales, the boot and shoe manufacturer, various trees, and 50 park seats (of caste iron with wooden slats as seen in the picture) given by leading townsmen.

52. This strange building in Pudsey Park was the result of a creditable desire by Pudsey's Local Board of Health to retain at least something of the town's old parsonage when it was demolished in 1894. The old parsonage stood just to the east of the present cenotaph. It had been built by Pudsey's famous 17th century puritan minister, Elkanah Wales and had the date 1647 on its decorative plasterwork. In 1832 it was replaced by a new parsonage, now Beckfield Retirement Home. For some years before its demolition the old parsonage was known as 'old Sally Fawberts' after its nonagenarian tenant. The porch and windows of the old house were rebuilt in the park as a façade to a small building intended as a mens' shelter. However, the damp soon resulted in it being relegated to a lumber room. It was later made into an aviary but was found inadequate for its new role. There was no dissension when the decision was made to replace it with a purpose built aviary.

53. The park shelter was not included in the original gifts for the park but given in 1897 by Mr. Thomas Lund of Crawshaw Mills. In front was a broad promenade with steps leading down to the bandstand. This became a popular rendezvous on Sunday afternoons. Previously a favourite Sunday afternoon resort had been the new cemetery 'to enjoy the fresh air and pleasant view, the growing beauties and the ornamental features of the place'. On Sunday evenings it was young people who 'prommed' in the park, at least until the gates shut at 8 p.m. when the 'prom' continued along Church Lane. This photograph was taken soon after the shelter was built.

54. Pudsey's first purpose built Mechanics Institute was opened in November 1880 by the Prime Minister's son, Mr. Herbert Gladstone. It was an ambitious scheme. The site, part of the old Waver Green, cost £1,600 and the building itself, designed by Hope and Jardine of Bradford, cost a further £3,000. In 1900 a new £4,000 extension was built, seen at the far right hand end of the building (see 55). But the main purpose of the Mechanics Institute was already eroding away as state education became compulsary and free. Moreover as a social centre the Mechanics Institute was threatened by the growth of political clubs. A Technical and Secondary School were opened in the new wing in 1905 but in response to pressure from the county authorities it soon moved to new premises in Richardshaw Lane. This left the Mechanics Institute with spare accommodation and a debt of £8,000. After much heart searching the officials had little option but to accept the Pudsey Council's offer to take over both the debt and the building. The interior was extensively remodelled by a local firm, Messrs. Jowett and Kendall, at a cost of £9,000, and reopened as Pudsey Town Hall in February 1912.

55. The foundation stone of the extension to the Mechanics Institute was laid by Pudsey's first mayoress, Mrs. James Stillings, on 5th September 1900. (The picture shows Mrs. Stillings on the platform facing the crowd.) She was the daughter of W.D. Scales, the Pudsey boot and shoe manufacturer of Grove House, and was remembered as a homely approachable woman. Although a Wesleyan she was also a good friend to the local Salvation Army. An especially memorable occasion was one Christmas when she invited 50 'old women' to her home, Radcliffe House, and led them in singing Christmas carols in the conservatory. Her husband was 'proud, sedate, reserved', 'a real gentleman', a man whose 'word was law', qualities which made him the unanimous choice for Pudsey's first mayor. As W.D. Scales had no sons, James Stillings continued the Scales' family business with his brother-in-law, Jonathan Webster. In 1910 he formed his own company, 'Stirlings Ltd'. In the background of the photograph is the clock tower of the Methodist's year old Trinity chapel.

56. The gentlemen about to set off in a fine 'carriage and pair' are probably members of the Pudsey Council. Carriages could be hired from Cabby Wood on Cemetery Road although leading families, such as the Stillings, the Huggans and the Forrests had their own. Cabby Wood's horses were also used for funerals and for pulling the fire engine. They were normally kept in a field and were not always amenable to being caught. And then it was said: 'There were no hurrying a funeral horse.' Behind the carriage is the entrance to the 1900 extension to the Mechanics Institute. The five men in front seem to be members of the Volunteers, dressed in their bottle green uniforms.

PROCLAMATION OF KING GEORGE V. READ AT PUDSEY 11TH MAY 1910.

57. The proclamation of King George V on 11th May 1910. The crowd is packed into the Recreation Ground to hear the mayor, Alderman Walter Forrest, read the proclamation. He is supported on the platform by town councillors and other local dignitaries. In days before radio and television it was traditional for news to be spread by work of mouth so that national events became adopted as local civic occasions. How many people would have the enthusiasm for such an event today? In the evening following the proclamation of the new king the death of the old king, Edward VII, was marked by a peel on the deeply muffled bells of Pudsey Church.

58. Pudsey's cenotaph was dedicated by the bishop of Bradford in 1922 before a crowd of almost 15,000. The 35 feet high monument in Portland stone commemorates the 333 Pudsey men killed in the 1914-1918 war. The architects were Messrs. Brierley and Rutherford of York whilst the bronze figure of a private of the West Yorkshire Regiment was the work of Henry Poole of London. Immediately before the dedication the bronze figure, which had been covered with a Union Jack, was unveiled by Pudsey's mayor, Councillor E.J. Byrd. The four tablets containing the names of those who died were similarly unveiled by children of the fallen. The cenotaph stands on the site of the east end of the old All Saints chapel of ease which was demolished in 1879. The steps on the south side however, reach out into the old graveyard. Bones recovered during the excations were collected and sealed in a vault beneath the memorial. A lead coffin encased in brick was left intact. Most of the old tombstones were removed to St. Lawrence churchyard.

59. Pudsey's first baby clinic opened in 1922 in the Town Hall crypt. The bonny baby prize winners here are posing at the back of the Secondary School, now Grangefield School, having had the prizes presented by the mayor, Councillor Fred Coe. 'Parky Wright', the mace bearer is at the back on the right. He retired as mace bearer in 1928 but remained as park keeper where he continued to command a healthy respect from generations of children. In 1928 the baby clinic moved to St. Lawrence House in the park which had been given by Councillor John Ben Ward and was opened by the Duke and Duchess of York.

IN THE CHILDREN'S PLAYGROUND, PUDSEY.

COPYRIGHT
PDY. 8.

LILYWHITE LTD
TRIANGLE HALIFAX

60. The children's playground was opened in April 1928 by the Duke and the Duchess of York, the present Queen Mother. They were the first members of the Royal Family to visit Pudsey. In addition to opening the children's playground they also opened the St. Lawrence baby clinic and laid the foundation stone of the Pudsey baths. Crowds packed the royal route and the church bells rang out. The playground, on the site of the derelict recreation ground, was equipped with a paddling pool, sandpit, shelter, refreshment kiosk, slides, swings and roundabouts through the generousity of Councillor John Ben Ward. It was designed by an octagenarian, Mr. Wickstead of Kettering, whose work Councillor Ward had seen and admired. Pudsey's playground was for years the mecca for thousands of children travelling into the town by tram. Perhaps the local paper was justified in its claim that 'Pudsey Playground has no equal in the North of England'.

Baths, Pudsey.

61. As the Duke and Duchess of York approached the market place to lay the foundation stone of Pudsey's public baths in April 1928, a 'lusty Yorkshire cheer' issued from the crowd, especially from the 1,400 flag waving schoolchildren. Local girl guides, under their captains the Misses L. and N. Miller, and boy scouts, under their scout master 'Johnny' Lingard, formed a guard of honour for the royal couple. The baths were opened the following June by the mayor, Councillor George Womersley. The 17 stone chairman of the Baths committee, Councillor Simeon Myers, provided a memorable climax to the occasion by publically diving in and being the first person to swim a length. The architect was Pudsey's Borough Surveyor, Basil H. Noble and the cost £14,000. It was designed as a dual purpose building, in the winter being converted into the Albert Hall by laying a dance floor over the pool. Above the stage is the Pudsey Coat of Arms, allowed by the College of Heralds in 1900, the year of the town's incorporation.

62. This charabanc load of children from Waterloo Infant School are all set for an outing, probably to Sunnyvale Gardens at Hipperholme. At this time, about 1920, the school used the Mount Tabor Sunday School, just to the left of the picture. Children went at three years old, staying until they were six when they went to Greenside School. The two teachers are Mrs Strickland and Miss Ashton. The children all look well wrapped up against the English summer. The solid tyres would make a bumpy ride, but perhaps a 'chara' was an improvement on a horse-drawn 'waggonette' which would have taken the children ten years earlier. The charabancs were nicknamed 'toastracks' because every other panel opened as a door. During the week the charabanc body was taken off the chassis and replaced by a waggon body for more mundane jobs. Notice the iron hoops hanging outside the house on the right. Every self-respecting child was an expert at bowling a hoop, usually iron ones for boys and wooden ones for girls.

63. What a shame we can't see the other side of this barrel organ which is causing such excitement in Chapeltown. Barrel organs, or tingalaries, could be hired daily from Leeds. This one is apparently publicising some of the Conservative Club's social events. Judging by the cloche hats worn by some of the women this must have been in the 1920s. The house on the right is Joseph Parker's watchmaker and jeweller's shop (see 18). The building at the back survived as a hairdresser and barber's shop until a few years ago. About the time of this photograph the local branch of the Association of Barbers was considering raising the price of a shave from 1d to 1½d despite some unease at the effect on trade of the new safety razor.

Pudsey Lifeboat Saty July 20th 1907

64. Lifeboat Saturday July 1907. In 1907 Pudsey's Lifeboat Committee planned to make the town's Lifeboat Saturday into a real carnival. It was a spectacular success. At the centre of the procession was the Worthing lifeboat, manned by the Scarborough lifeboat crew and drawn by seven splendidly harnessed horses from William Barraclough and Co. of Providence Ironfounders at Stanningley. The Boys Brigade Band, the Stanningley Band and the Pudsey Borough Band provided the music for the procession of private carriages, the Nursing Association, the British Womens' Temperance Association, St. John's Ambulance, local Friendly Societies and the Pudsey Fire Brigade. The procession moved along the gaily decorated streets, along Chapeltown, Fartown, Littlemoor and Richardshaw Lane to Leigh Mills dam. Here the lifeboat was launched, down a nine feet drop, which soaked everybody, including the mayor. The profit on the day of £90 was considered 'very satisfactory'. This picture was taken in Chapeltown.

65. Pudsey Feast in 1915. The Feast was the highlight of Pudsey's year. Local butchers worked overtime slaughtering scores of oxen for the 'tide beef' whilst the women busied themselves making hundreds of thousands of Pudsey feast tarts. It was the time for important local cricket matches, and outings to the seaside. Most especially it was when all the paraphernalia of the feast trundled up Lowtown to the Recreation Ground. The feast was held here from 1880 when the Local Board bought the Junction Field for the town (the feast had to move from its earlier site when Lowtown Station was built on it) until 1928 when the Recreation Ground was converted into a children's playground. Vicker's theatre, Scott's menagerie, the cockerills and the shamrock (the steam swing boats which can just be seen at the back left of the photograph) and many other attractions all helped to make Pudsey's feast the best for miles around.

66. Pudsey's carnival was revived in 1923 by the mayor, Councillor Richard Ingham. Inspired by Blackpool's carnival he determined that Pudsey should have one too. Within just one month Pudsey organised a carnival which attracted a crowd of almost 50,000 to see the mile long procession. Shops, houses and whole streets were gay with streamers, flags and mottos, whilst Lowtown was said to 'rival a scene in fairyland'. There was a profit of £400 (Blackpool's carnival cost the town £10,000 that year) which was divided between Pudsey's Cinderella Fund and the District Nursing Association. Thereafter the Pudsey carnival became an annual event until the Second World War. This picture shows a later mayor, Councillor Simeon Myers in carnival mood in the rose bedecked mayoral car. The mace bearer, 'Parky Wright' sits in front (see 59).

67. The Moravian Sunday School float is well supported as it sets out to join the Pudsey carnival procession. Sam. B. Wood, a Pudsey man who became a well-known composer of brass band music wrote a song especially for Pudsey's carnival: *There's a little spot, beating all the lot,/ And it's not beside the sea,/ Carnival is there, laughter ev'ry where,/ Pudsey is the place for you and me!.../ Come along to Pudsey for the Carnival,/ Come along to Pudsey right away./ Ev'ryone is happy at the carnival,/ Come along and join the fun today./ All around the streamers will by flying,/ And ev'rybody shouting on the way,/ Hurrah by gum it's champion!/ At the Pudsey carnival today.*

68. The Primrose Buds' float is assembled in the grounds of Grove House, the home of Mr. Alfred Lund of Crawshaw Mill. It is about to move to the Recreation Ground where the entries gathered for the carnival procession. The Primrose Buds was the Conservative's organisation for girls. The boys' equivalent was the Young Britons. Most of the mothers were in the Primrose League. After weeks of preparation everything is ready and the party poses proudly to have its photograph taken. Only the horse looks dejected and fed up with the fuss. This year the Primrose Buds won first prize.

THE NEED OF THE HOUR

TEMPERANCE

69. Here is yet another carnival float, this time already assembled in the Recreation Ground. Hutton Terrace can be seen in the background. In the 1920s the triple alliance of religious nonconformity, political liberalism and temperance was still strong. Pudsey had an active branch of the British Womens' Temperance Association and most chapels had their own Bands of Hope where children were expected to 'sign the pledge' of total abstinence. The Methodist's Lower Sunday School Band of Hope was especially popular, not least because of its cosily warm coke stove in the middle of the room. The group in the photograph is from Robin Lane Primitive Methodists whose chapel, built in 1900, is now the Methodist's St. Andrews Church.

70. An Idyll by Black Carr Woods. Summer strolls in Fulneck valley, especially on Sunday evenings after evening service were once quite an institution. This part of the valley used to be known as 'Happy Valley' as about sixty years ago there were plans to develop it as pleasure gardens, in the manner of Shipley Glen. The bridge crosses the beck, the ancient parish and township boundary, into Black Carr woods. Most of the trees are oak or silver birch and in spring before they come into leaf the ground is carpeted with bluebells. Celandine, wood anenomies, wood sorrel, pink purslane, kingcups and milkmaids (or cuckoo flower) also grow here. This is still a popular walk but today the skirts and footwear of the ladies in the photograph would be disastrous, even in summer.

Tong Bridge Pudsey

71. The next three photographs are taken in Fulneck valley, about half a mile down stream from Black Carr woods. This lane from Pudsey across the valley to Tong also used to be a popular walk, especially for courting couples and for Sunday afternoon strolls to see the peacocks in Tong churchyard. An old stone causeway survives alongside much of the lane and this, together with the rich variety of shrubs in the hedgerows, suggests it is a very ancient 'way'. On the Tong side it is called Keeper Lane, after the gamekeeper's cottage at the top. An old name for the lane on the Pudsey side is Abe Lane. This is probably named after Abraham Hutchinson who in the 18th century lived at what is now Newstead House adjoining the lane. Another name is Pyg Lane. The bridge over the beck used to be called Hobroyd Bridge. The name is taken from an adjacent field on the Tong side called Hobroyd which means the clearing in the wood where hobgoblins lurk. The narrow bridge over Keeper Lane in the distance carried a tramway linking Bowling Iron Works with Alexandra pit which was about half a mile to the left of the picture.

4551. FULNECK FROM TONG VALLEY.

72. Here is Fulneck Golf Course, probably in the early 1920s, looking from the valley towards the Moravian settlement. You might think it does not look much like a golf course, but in the early days golf courses were rarely the groomed, single-purpose tracks of land they are today. The fairways were often relatively narrow lanes mown through growing crops, and the hedges served as additional hazards. At first the 'playing season' at Fulneck finished in April to restart in August when the hay harvest was in. The Club, founded in 1892, was the inspiration of Reverend Titterington, the headmaster of the Fulneck Boys' School. In the background the line of 'The Terrace' is not yet complete. The gap at the far end was soon to be filled by an extension to the Girls' School.

73. Fulneck valley in 1903, seen from the Tong side of
Hobroyd Bridge. What is immediately noticeable is
how much better kept the walls and causeway were
then, although recently the Tong Cockersdale Volunteers have begun a mammoth programme of restora-
tion. The beck, flowing down the valley from the left,
is said to have contained trout before it became
polluted, first with dyewater from Gibraltar mill and
then more drastically by the Smalewell sewage works.
Just in front of the mown hayfield is Dyehouse Lane,
made by the Moravians on first coming to Pudsey to
reach their dyehouse by the beck. The Moravians also
built a bathhouse adjoining the dyehouse pond. There
were strict regulations for its use, brethren and sisters
using it on alternate days and those suffering from
sores going in last. In the extreme top right is Sisters
Wood. Although obviously renamed by the Moravians,
it was there long before the Moravians came, previously being known as Holdsworth's Wood. In the 17th
century the Holdsworth family owned the extensive
Bankhouse estate of which all this land was part.

74. This cluster of cottages is probably on the site of the old hamlet of Ulversthorpe. The name fell into disuse at least 500 years ago and by the 18th century the hamlet was known as Lane End. Today the district is called Bankhouse. A group of Moravians came to live here in 1742 before their new settlement was built about a quarter of a mile away (see 22). One of the cottages on the left, now demolished, had the initials SH carved on the door lintel. They stood for Samuel Hillas, a yeoman clothier who was the first Pudsey man to be received into the Moravian church. Many of the Moravians' early preachings and 'singing hours' were at his house. In the distance is the 'Spite Tower', built by Joseph Gaunt of the Bankhouse Inn, in 1872. It is said that Joseph Gaunt had some feud with Colonel Plumbe Tempest who lived across the valley at Tong Hall and that he built the tower to spoil Colonel Tempest's view.

75. The previous photograph is taken from about where this smartly dress man is standing. He is coming down from Greentop, the traditional site of Pudsey's bonfires to celebrate great national events. In 1911 a local architect, William Shackleton, had the task of building the 30 feet high bonfire for George V's coronation. 160 gallons of tar and oil ensured a spectacular blaze. Scores of other bonfires could be seen in every direction, whilst it was said the light from Pudsey's fire could be seen from the Lancashire border to York. The picture shows Bankhouse well springing from the hillside. This probably accounts for the siting here of the ancient settlement of Ulversthorpe. The well survives today but is not so well kept, nor is the causeway in front. In the trees to the left is Nesbit Hall. This originated as Bank House, the centre of a large estate. Most of the house was rebuilt in the mid-18th century. It was subsequently owned by the Nisbet family for over 50 years and gradually acquired the name Nesbit Hall. The changed spelling presumably reflects local reluctance to struggle with the pronounciation of 'Nisbet'.

76. Few Pudsey children today are able to enjoy the fun, and sweet smells of a hayfield. At haytime it was a case of many hands make light work, although this scene is somewhat leisurely. The children seem to be on their way home from school. After mowing the hay was tossed with forks to dry it, raked into rows, and then into haycocks as seen here. Then the hay was made into a huge haystack and finally thatched against the weather. This field, part of Samuel Moss' farm at Wood Nook, is now lost under the new ring road. Less regretfully the forest of Stanningley's mill chimneys, seen in the distance, too has gone. Perhaps this is an appropriate photograph with which to end the book. It reflects the partnership between the textile industry and agriculture, continuing well into this century, which for at least 600 years was the foundation of Pudsey's prosperity.